BUSINESS
THE DONE THING

Drusilla Beyfus
Cartoons by Austin

Ebury Press · London

First published 1993

1 3 5 7 9 10 8 6 4 2

Text copyright © Drusilla Beyfus 1993
Illustrations copyright © David Austin 1993
Drusilla Beyfus has asserted her right under the Copyright,
Designs and Patents Act, 1988, to be identified as the author of
this work.

All rights reserved. No part of this publication may be
reproduced, stored in a retrieval system, or transmitted in any
form or by any means, electronic, mechanical, photocopying,
recording or otherwise, without prior permission of the
copyright owners.

First published in the United Kingdom in 1993 by
Ebury Press Limited
Random House, 20 Vauxhall Bridge Road, London SW1V 2SA

Random House Australia (Pty) Limited
20 Alfred Street, Milsons Point, Sydney,
New South Wales 2061, Australia

Random House New Zealand Limited
18 Poland Road, Glenfield
Auckland 10, New Zealand

Random House South Africa (Pty) Limited
PO Box 337, Bergvlei, South Africa

Random House UK Limited Reg. No 954009

A CIP catalogue record for this book
is available from the British Library

ISBN 0 09 177059 9

Filmset by SX Composing Ltd, Rayleigh, Essex

Printed in England by Clays Ltd, St Ives plc

To Angela

Contents

Preface 8 Interview Ahead 10

Team Work 15 Suited 19

Blunder Boss 22 Chief Woman 25

Present Rites 28 One Down 30

Scents and Sensibility 32

Dismissal 34

Correct Forms of Address 37

Your Ten-Thirty 39 On The Line 41

Dear Answering Machine 44

Smoking Issues 46 Staff Jolly 50

Dos and Don'ts 53 No! 56

My Apologies 57 Excuses 60

Preface

The news that some big companies are thinking of introducing de-stressing courses for pressurised employees and executives prompted my radical thought: why not try studies in good manners?

It is my belief that a courteous approach in the workplace can be a balm, a blessing and a way round a thousand and one stressful situations. Practitioners stand to gain a golden advantage. Not only does courtesy belong to the moral 'oughts', but much evidence shows that it is appreciated in terms understood in the market place. In common with free-range hens, humans who are treated well respond by producing the quality egg.

Common sense alone suggests that any employee whose job brings him or her in contact with the public needs to call on ways of dealing tactfully with customers. The punters would surely react with relief to personnel who believed in politeness. As a bonus, the reputation of the firm might soar, and not a penny more spent on P.R. or advertising. And this is merely the hard-nosed case.

In the field of business entertaining, company dos, and even in the administrative arrangements for meetings, knowing how to make people feel welcome is a time-honoured attribute of the good host, whether he or she is acting in a professional or private capacity.

If further proof were needed of the practical value of a

sense of diplomacy, it might be witnessed in the whole hotch-potch of relationships between the sexes at work. Office manners are in the making as far as the male attitude to women as equals, subordinates and chiefs is concerned. An awareness of the circumstances is called for, as some women are happy to have the door opened on their behalf, whereas others may object on principle to a form of etiquette they consider outmoded.

So many areas could do with a brisk debriefing on civility. Language springs to mind at once. A largely unrecognised disadvantage embedded in the everyday use of expletives is the loss of a *bona fide* verbal outlet. With few or no language taboos left to break, what is a poor soul to do when he or she wishes to express signal fury or outrage? Ensuring that fewer F-words found their way into circulation might count as relief work.

Political correctness represents a further threat to human communication now that 'outplacement counselling' is what happens instead of the sack. In attempting to adopt euphemisms in order to protect people from hearing the hard truth, the depths to which the whitewash has gone has managed to bring the kind impulses that lay behind the diplomatic fib ('He's decided to take a sabbatical' . . . 'I can't. I'm working late every night') into disrepute.

The pill that has to be swallowed by those who wish to hang on to life's civilities is the prevailing school of thought that good manners and the market place are incompatible. Showing consideration has little or no place, goes the refrain, in a competitive world where personal ambition, power broking and the ruthless demands of efficiency are paramount.

But other voices are being heard. As manners are minor morals, they may have a renewed place in the sun within the moral framework that people are said to feel the lack of.

Granted, haste is an enemy of politeness – it does take a moment out to say hello, thank you or sorry. But if the goal is more of a challenge, so be it. This may even be one of the rewards. When someone makes it in this hard world who is reputed to be well-liked, that redounds enormously to his or her credit.

The American novelist Ernest Hemingway once remarked that 'courage was grace under pressure'. The same might often be said of courtesy.

Interview Ahead

Doing well at the job interview calls for a polishing-up of social skills. Success may not depend on it, but good manners make a favourable impression as well as helping their possessor to remain in control in a hot seat. More than that, the interviewer may recognise that someone with a sense of the appropriate should be able to discern the difference between a sparky idea that is effective and a loopy idea that flops.

The best approach, as ever, is to be properly prepared. First impressions do count. One recommendation here is to go to the bother of staging an actual rehearsal of the likely procedures at the encounter between candidate and interviewer. A friend might be cast as the latter. Go through all the moves from the beginning: opening the door of the room occupied by an interrogator, entering the space with an air of confidence well this side of cockiness, shaking hands or, if none is proffered, confining greetings to a verbal exchange, waiting to be asked to sit down, taking up an alert stance in the chair, facing the interviewer, maintaining eye contact with him or her. The practise could extend to a run-through of prepared answers to standard questions of the 'why-do-you-wish-to-work-for-this-company?' order. Never over-rehearse as it will stifle spontaneity; besides, nobody wishes to employ an automaton.

Mannerisms need watching as in the usual way they provide comfort at a tense moment. Hair-twiddling, foot-twitching, nose-stroking, may be read as signs of an overly nervous disposition. No smoking at the interview, it goes without saying. An exception might be if a cigarette was offered, though smokers are advised to decline with thanks, as indulging the foible is a distraction.

Advice on business attire is suggested elsewhere in this little volume, but certain points need mentioning specifically in connection with interview choices. Whether one likes it or not, in some bastions of tradition, the following preferences have come to be looked on unfavourably. For males, these include brown shoes with city suits, an open-necked shirt, a handbag-like shoulder bag, hair swept into a ponytail, wearing one gold earring, carrying a ballpoint pen in the breast pocket. For women, the proscriptions consist of a blouse unbuttoned one button too far, startling jewellery, a punkish hairdo, a micro-skirt. A word has to be added about a lady in trousers. Perfectly acceptable if the post is in the more liberally-minded branches of the arts, the media, publishing, advertising or the entertainment industries, or where conditions demand. Caution is called for, though, for those after a job in the senior professions. Females who like to wear trousers, notwithstanding the high fashion rating of the style, may be deemed inappropriately attired for a position that involves dealing with clients in person.

The general informality of styles of address in everyday life meets its come-uppance at many a job interview. Keep to the formal approach as a golden rule. It is 'Mister So-and-So' or 'Miss Such-and-Such' in conversation. An exception might be if the interviewer introduces himself or herself in first-name only terms. If so, follow that form.

Replies to questions about pastimes or interests outside working hours are tricky, because it is difficult to

*Try to overcome your natural modesty.
You're here to talk about yourself.*

predict which of the remotely realistic answers might strike a sympathetic hearing. Any undertaking which suggests shouldering some responsibility or a show of initiative is promising. For example, helping to set up a college sponsored swim or manning a charity shop would be worth mentioning, but a two-week stint distributing sales leaflets might well fall on stony ears.

Any discussion about the employer's industry, company or organisation is liable to reveal who has done his or her homework. In the case of any position that requires more than routine skills, doing research on the background of an employer's business is rarely a waste of time. House journals, company reports, recruitment literature – even the corporate notice board are all grist.

As to stated motives for wishing to join up, a hint of

genuine enthusiasm is rarer than might be imagined.

A watchword at all times is to sell yourself agreeably. A mood of self-deprecation and mock modesty is liable to be accepted at face value and irony ignored. So toot your own trumpet.

One of the most sensitive aspects of the Q and A session may be probes to which the candidate does not wish to give a full or wholly honest answer. 'Do you plan on having a family?' may be a point put to members of either sex. Many have found the only recourse lies in diplomatic fibbing, justified perhaps by a genuine doubt as to the truthful reply, or the belief that the probe is discriminatory.

Interview mythology is full of cheeky incidents that saved the day. The author recalls an example in which E., who had applied for a post as an editorial assistant, had done quite well at the interview but came into the category of a just-miss contender. As the candidate hovered by the door on her way out she suddenly wheeled round and returned to the fray. Declaring 'I know you are not going to offer me the job', she asked one favour. Would we tell her exactly why? The post was hers.

When there is little to be lost, an act of chutzpah might be spot on.

Don't be late.

Team Work

Playing the part that is expected of you in a team of associates depends as much as anything on getting along with fellow members. The mantra of fitting in is especially important in any effort in which members are interdependent. As a criteria it tends to apply across the board, from dum-dums to clever clogs, from newcomers to the most experienced, though it is far from an exact science.

Before readers suspect that this amounts to a recommendation for grey conformity, it must first be said that many are those whose face failed to fit who live to become pillars of support in other comparable ventures.

The problem for many may be how to play the part without denting your self-respect. Whereas it would be misleading to suggest that a courteous approach is a passport to acceptance from the rest of the team, what can be said is that showing consideration generally helps to make people feel better, happier and consequently more productive. Good manners certainly make the daily round a little sweeter and more salubrious. However, only an idealist would imagine that courtesy will be universally appreciated in a world in which office politics are cheerfully accounted to be savage.

Considered below are recommendations for dealing

with some sensitive spots in the everyday cut and thrust of team work.

Teams thrive on the individual member feeling appreciated. Thus, ignoring an associate unintentionally is a renowned source of miff. Cutting people intentionally, of course, has always offended against etiquette.

Part of the charm of uttering a friendly greeting or showing some sign of recognition of a workmate's presence is that such a small gesture can help to dispel the atmosphere of anonymity that can cloud the day's prospects. The fellowly act may be specially appreciated by someone who is feeling left out or low.

Exercising rights over personal territory in the building requires some recognition of other people's sensitivities if your claims are to be respected. To take a small example, annexing an associate's desk space by plonking your clobber, papers, files and what-have-you on their square of space is easily done, no doubt, but the act often seems symbolic and can cause resentment. A guideline is to keep your things to your side of the fence, or at least to apologise for being a bad neighbour.

Whilst we are on the topic, it must be said that for a colleague to return from a break to find another member at his or her desk is a profound breach of courtesy. Office managers please note. However, if the offender is no more than a cuckoo, asking pleasantly if he or she would move their things is likely to expedite the process faster than giving rein to the irritation, not to say anger, that

*The office politics certainly is cut-throat.
I'm his tea-taster.*

may be sparked in proprietorially-minded beasts. But suppose the original occupant has been sacked and the new tenant is placed by chance in the unhappy position of having to break the news? Expressions of sympathy may sound hypocritical if the appointee is known to have coveted the sacked person's post. One may always express regrets as the successor at the methods involved and offer to make the changeover as painless as possible.

The sheer dailiness of working together depends for smooth running on the minutiae of office admin. Therefore, those noble souls who bother to replenish supplies of fax paper, paper clips, envelopes or coffee before the last consignment runs out, who think to report a faulty machine, take a generous view of the chore of washing up long-neglected coffee mugs or drinking glasses, or take care of lost property, do more than their bit as saviours of the working environment.

Joining in, in general, is all part of *esprit de corps*. However, many associates prefer to sit on the sidelines as spectators rather than participants, which need be no reflection on their professional skills. It does count in the social field, though. Loners might consider making some compensatory effort if they don't wish to take part in corporate festivities. Notwithstanding a decision to bunk off the office party, it would be thoughtful to contribute to any collection for a team member, or even to offer to help with any preparations for a collective jolly.

Personal confidences are quite another aspect of sharing. How far ought you to keep mum about an associate's private infidelities, office romance, state of health, emotional crises or attempts to oust a colleague from a post? Gossip, one of the rewards of team engagement, would certainly be a lot duller if a blanket of circumspection descended on the dialogue. Yet reputations can be lost on the grapevine. A guideline is a developed sense of the difference between lighthearted speculation intended to entertain and malicious comment that may carry a serious risk to the subject. Perhaps the best litmus test in this ambivalent situation is one of personal loyalty.

Another point applies to users of computers with the system that enables personal messages to be flashed up on the screen of the recipient. Wonderful as a means of conversation that can never be overheard, undoubtedly, but a potential source of embarrassment as well. Open-plan offices and casualness about usage mean that the ribald/mischievous/hurtful/denigratory comment that was intended for private delectation alone can all too easily be scanned by an unintended reader. Swiftly blanking out the message is now an etiquette command.

Suited

Masculine conservatism in dress was well summed up by a male observer, wearing a jacket and trousers of light hue, who attended a reception for notables. Surveying a crowded scene in which every man present was attired in a dark, uniformly city suit, he reflected ruefully that to look at them, 'the Sixties might just as well never have happened'. But our observer was in the City.

Almost as sharp as the old class divisions are the distinctions between the suited and the informally-attired rest. Occupation and status still determine levels of acceptability. Generally, in fields of employment in which employees deal with the public, or whose job entails representing the organisation, the custom of wearing collar and necktie is pretty well absolute.

However, those who are disinclined to have their stylish wings clipped can take comfort from the relaxation of a number of taboos at the workplace. The suits reign, as we have said, but the cut, style and fabric can

That tie is rather Bohemian, Withers.

reflect the wearer's taste. Jackets may be *de rigueur*, but they could be in leather or in a knit. Neck-tie design has blossomed, some might say with a vengeance. In arty and media circles occasional sports caps have become exceptions to the etiquette that a man removes his headgear indoors. The long and the short of the divisive hairstyle debate has been resolved in many erstwhile pockets of conservatism on the basis that if the head looks groomed, fine.

Limits are probably not of as great matter for women, but many a woman wonders if she can get away with jeans and a handy sweater when the boss generally dons a suit. Very probably the dissentor would be thought over-casual in the majority of cases – especially if their job involves meeting clients or representing the company. In any event, it is always wisest to test the waters before introducing change or innovation in accepted customs in dress.

Exceptions to the sea of grey suits and white shirts are numerous, but they tend to be concentrated in big cities and to focus on arty circles, the entertainment and music industries, and the creative echelons of the media. Here, if the boss wears a leather jacket and open-necked attire, it can be assumed that he or she is unlikely to object to subordinates following suit.

Some sensitivity has to be shown by a male traditionalist who finds himself in alien waters in which casual clothes are the norm. He may risk being mistaken for a bit of a wally if he turns up clad in Dad's British warm.

Members eligible to sport old school ties, club ties, or college or regimental ties won't need any advice on when to wear them. A point might be made though that a certain reserve is noticeable about wearing the symbol of allegiance to an institution in the company of those who do not share these loyalties. Where the sign is recognised and appreciated, obviously no such reservations apply.

In an uncertain picture, a few maxims apply. Appropriate dress denotes respect. A spark of individuality in attire shows self-respect. Looking good is never a bad thing.

Finally it should be said that worn and shabby clothes may well have a place now where before they raised eyebrows, but this is all a question of degree. Mucky apparel, worn from choice, has few friends.

Blunder Boss

If bosses ever give pause to wonder why their secretaries wear such a despondent mien or have a surly manner, they might reflect upon whether a few errors have not crept into their own performance. For whatever else the boss/secretary association is proverbially noted for, extra-curricular politeness on the side of the senior party rarely features.

The difficulty as often as not is the old one of communication skills. It is axiomatic that many chiefs lack the ability to jump into the skin of the person on the receiving end of their instructions. What compounds the secretarial dilemma is the imbalance in her (the subject is usually female) relatively lowly standing in the company; as the put-upon member she is especially dependent on friendly and courteous behaviour, if only for the sake of her self-esteem.

The case in mitigation of the tactless or boorish boss, that business is business and there is no time for niceties, doesn't hold water in the end. Personal aggravation impairs efficiency, stifles good will and is likely to leave the boss abandoned once too often by the wiser secretary.

From many a secretarial desk come reminders of the ways of going on liable to cause umbrage among those whose job it is to 'take-a-letter-Pam'. What drives many

secretaries round the twist are some of the practices mentioned below.
- Telling you to do something without even glancing in your direction or saying please and thank you.
- Shouting commands while you are on the telephone obeying instructions.
- Being clockwatched over the lunch break by a boss to whom two-hour lunches are habitual.
- Accusing you of losing important documents when he/she was responsible for the lapse, for which he/she neglects to offer apologies.
- Walking off without leaving word about where he or she may be or the hour at which a return is on the cards.
- Watching you take it easy during the day before deciding to dictate long memos and letters that must be typed a twink before going home time.
- Spelling simple words and repeating the date as if you were daft.
- Refusing to open a door or to offer a helping hand as you stagger out piled high with samples.
- Declining to take personal messages for you, however important the content may be.
- Keeping clients with appointments waiting unnecessarily on the basis that you will smooth things over.
- Showing little interest in using you to your full capacity on the basis that you are 'just a secretary'.
- Assuming that part of the job is to undertake personal services such as tidying up after him/her, booking, can-

It's being in charge that means never having to say sorry.

celling and rebooking hair appointments, being sent out shopping, washing-up drinking glasses and mugs.

The last point about personal service is worth dwelling on. One female boss known to the author mentioned that when the word coffee crops up in meetings, she positively pounces on the coffee percolator in order to do the honours herself, so sensitive has the issue become between her and her secretary.

Bosses of either sex can get round this issue with a measure of common sense and courtesy. Ways in which the score can be equalled may be through acts of personal generosity which are more than perks. Attentive kindnesses might be nearer the mark. Known examples range from the loan of music or sound equipment, handing over the car keys for the occasional use of the secretary, tickets for Wimbledon or the theatre, or invitations to a good party. Whatever form the token thank-you takes, it should signify a gesture between equals.

Chief Woman

Many a subordinate male who works for a woman boss feels uncertain about how to treat her in a social role. Despite the fact that there are numerous males whose entire working life has been spent with women as superiors, there remain niggling areas of doubt about the niceties.

It is a tricky subject about which to generalise because of the wide spectrum of women's attitudes, and the overriding consideration of the occupation concerned. Usually, though, women do appreciate courteous behaviour from everyone, including men. What may be objected to is that form of etiquette which seems very stiff and makes a public palaver over such gestures as opening a door for a woman to go through, ahead of the males. If it can be done naturally, well and good, if not, let it pass, is the rule.

Doubts tend to be sharpest in situations which are part social, part business. Take, as an example, an occasion when a male subordinate is invited to a working lunch or dinner by his female chief. He has a dual role to play. He is an associate, and also an escort. His best policy is to maintain the usual practice of being attentive. He should allow his boss to lead the way to the table and show him where to sit. He might pull out a chair for her (unless pre-empted by the waiter). It would be polite – as with any host, either male or female – to take a cue as to the cost of the dishes to order from the host's own choices from the menu, and to follow suit.

All the usual courtesies at table should be observed without officiously assuming the role of host. The man should refill his companion's glass before attending to his own, keep an eye on the general service and offer to remind the waiter of any delayed order, if need be. He could offer to light her cigarette in any case, but should be punctilious about asking her permission to smoke. Putting extras on the bill such as cigarettes for himself, or ordering drinks without being invited to, is off limits, as would be the case with any polite guest.

Keeping this side of familiarity, his role is to be agreeable company at the same time as proving himself a competent professional.

It would probably be a miscalculation to assume that the date indicated an interest in some form of sexual ploy at the close of business: males are protected by the same code as women on the harassment issue.

As to the wisdom of the male paying personal compliments, a safe policy is to desist. Many women are

It's a working lunch, to discuss cutting expenses.

averse on principle to forms of flattery based on their femininity, as they wish to be judged by professional skills only – as would a man. On the other hand, few people are immune to the charms of timely remarks about their competence, brilliance or professionalism.

Another service that our guest might undertake would be to offer to call or ring for a cab on behalf of his boss, and when it arrives to see her into her seat. Then again, it would be polite to walk her to her car, the bus stop, or whatever suits. If the occasion ends late in the evening, and the woman is unaccompanied, an offer to see her safely on her way home is only civil. Social kissing is unlikely, as a rule, but is worth a comment. Much is said about the inappropriateness of the gesture between colleagues. Oddly enough in some spheres including the author's, nothing is thought of a male chief opting to bid goodnight to a female subordinate with a kiss on the cheek. It is just unexceptional behaviour. Yet part of the blurred borderlines setting the tone of social customs between the sexes at work, is that such a gesture is liable to misinterpretation. In some circumstances, the male might be thought presumptuous or worse. On the other hand, if the female makes the first move, and she is the man's superior, only he can judge whether to duck or accept the brush of cheeks with good grace.

Present Rites

Round comes the manilla envelope yet again, collecting for a colleague's present. The rite of marking birthdays (especially the boss's), weddings, maternity leave, baby arrivals and benign departures with a tangible offering has become as much a part of office life as the company beano.

A touchy point of etiquette concerns acceptable apologies for bowing out of the procedure. The usual justification such as that you are impecunious or are disinclined to add to your already extensive list of present-expectant friends and family, cuts little mustard among those who have produced their readies.

Nevertheless, certain circumstances provide a polite

We're collecting for Joe, and yes you do have a choice.

way out. Among these might be: hardly knowing the prospective recipient from Adam, or not being known yourself to them. New arrivals, part-timers, casuals and people on the fringe could call on the fact without giving offence. An approach which offers a *bona fide* excuse between good friends is to withdraw from the collective offering on the grounds that you intend to produce a private offering. If valid, fine; if not, perhaps it was your good intention at the time.

On the allied point of whether it is acceptable to sign the greetings card that usually accompanies the loot without contributing any money, or turn up at any hospitality in connection with the offering, the answer must be in most cases – surely not.

One Down

Knowing how to respond to others' ups and downs on the corporate ladder can be as challenging as managing your own affairs. Few will have the nerve of an executive known to the author whose loyal chief had been replaced in a staff reshuffle. Finding himself in the new incumbent's office and surveying a drab scene from which all belongings had just been removed our head quipped, 'I see you have stamped your personality on the place overnight'.

On the other side of the coin, an ability to rise above pin-pricks and put-downs is an occupational must. One guiding principle as far as spoken or written barbs are concerned is to cap it if you can, or else ignore it. The latter course at least deprives the detractor of any satisfaction of knowing whether the shot reached home or misfired. Keeping smiling undoubtedly calls for bluff, but cultivating a 'that beat it smile' may be more effective than a riposte.

Handling spiky asides from friends and foes is one thing, dealing tactfully with professional rebuffs is quite another. Part of the difficulty in knowing how best to hold your own ground may be that there is nothing firm to go on, save the impression that you have lost ground or are under a cloud. Whether to raise the matter formally in these circumstances is open to doubt. The

*Claire will explain the rules of engagement
when seeking promotion.*

trouble is that once said the declaration cannot be retracted, and what may be nothing of moment hardens into a stated grievance. One way of testing the waters might be to suggest taking on new responsibilities – assuming the asker is in a position to act on an agreement. The official response might be an indication of the way the wind is blowing.

The strongest case in favour of exercising restraint is in any conflict of opinion about who or what was to blame for mistakes or failure. Remaining cool allows the suspect to stay in control, no mean achievement when under pressure.

Watchwords are: avoid rubbishing a colleague; if the dum-dum in the case is a member under your aegis, accept full responsibility for the muddle. Incidentally, if you have lucklessly done some damn silly thing which has not yet come to the attention of authority, one ploy is to drop a hint or two in advance as to the possibility of a cock-up without admitting to the full burden of it. In this way, if the worst occurs, the cutting edge will have been shaved off the shock value of the incident. If nothing untoward surfaces, you are in clover.

Being in and out of favour is so much part of corporate life that to be a participant is to run the risks. One compensation is a bond to which little recognition is given as one of the pleasures of office life — namely friendships. Not everyone melts away necessarily when the ice is thin.

Scents and Sensibility

It is in every sense all-pervasive. What may be done within the bounds of acceptability when an associate has a predilection for a make of scent or aftershave that literally gets up your nose?

The experience is easy to dismiss as trivial, but the strength of many so-called 'fragrances' splashed on the person with merry abandon can represent a taste gap that is a pain to live with at work.

Any direct comment by the disaffected would almost certainly cause umbrage: a wearer's favourite-scented

It's extraordinary how potent cheap perfume is.

lotion is highly personal and part of the way in which they like to present themselves. In any case, sensitive noses have to face the fact that the olfactory sense is subjective, and that a delectable perfume to one person may be distinctly malodorous to another.

If there is an answer it must surely lie in diplomatic hints, as candour on the topic risks giving offence. Obvious ruses such as window-opening (where this is a possibility), purposively using papers as a fan, nose-wrinkling, all seem to verge on rudeness. One way, which costs admittedly, is to produce an alternative make on the basis that this smell is really worth trying, as a present. Then again, some brave soul might mention a fact, which happens to be true, that one can never be sure how scent will respond when worn next to the skin.

Probably the best means is through the mediation of a pal of the offender. Perhaps he or she could pick a good moment to suggest that the perfume gives X or Y a headache.

Dismissal

A colleague who has been dismissed or made redundant can put friends and loyalists in a bit of a spot. They may be unsure as to whether the announcement should be treated as a form of bereavement or as a blip in a promising career graph. Understandably, few associates of the party know what is the best thing to do or say. A commonplace reaction, but one that scarcely helps the other, is to reflect ruefully that there, but for the grace of heaven knows who, go I.

As a very general rule, it can be assumed that people who are sacked don't want to dwell upon their demise with Tom, Dick and Harry — the very necessary exceptions being intimates.

It might be wiser to wait for the dismissed member to raise the topic, in preference to initiating a discussion which might be thought intrusive. Certainly, the moments following the delivery of the blow are no time to make enquiries about the victim's pay-off terms or redundancy money.

If someone wishes to express support and sympathy,

*I won't insult your intelligence with
euphemisms. You're fired.*

they should try to put as good a face on future prospects as credibility allows. Suggesting any useful contacts or leads would all be good to hear. Similarly, in times of stress, people always like to know they have been valued by their associates and work-mates.

The response of others is likely to be coloured by the particular: to be given the old heave-ho at twenty years old is regrettable, but hopefully there is plenty of time ahead. To be dismissed in middle-age very probably has life-changing implications. To be given the push within a few years of retirement is likely to narrow horizons horribly and prematurely.

As the practice of seeing dismissed staff off the premises on the day on which they are fired is far from exceptional, points go to those who can offer to help on the ground in a practical way. Helping to clear out a desk or filing cabinet, coping with anxieties about access to personal files stored in the computer system, and making a note of any forwarding address for mail, are all ways of showing consideration. If time and mood allow, offering to stand him or her a cheering one might not go amiss.

Not everyone who is dismissed wishes the word to go round as such. The much despised use of euphemisms may have a place if this applies. Suitable cover-ups could be that the departing member has decided to take a sabbatical, explore fresh fields, is hoping to gain further qualifications in their subject, or has belatedly recognised that marketing/selling/clerical work is not for him/her. Finally, from the viewpoint of the dismissed, one special point needs consideration. When the announcement comes as a shock, bursting into tears may not seem too strong a response. Despite the provocation, women (and men) are advised against crying on the job. Tears won't change anything, will almost certainly be thought unprofessional, and moreover are death to the appearance. Keeping one's dignity is a golden asset when assets may be in short supply. Better to retreat to the loo.

Correct Forms of Address

The instant intimacy of our times has upturned many certainties about how to address the boss, and the names by which colleagues are known.

On the one hand, first name terms prevail in many quarters where up until quite recently the rule of prefix and surname applied, or perhaps of surname only. On the other, in a business setting, where the commanding heights of employment often demand a correspondingly elevated form of address, such mateyness has distinct limits. Yet to get it wrong is to be considered either stuffy or over-familiar. So how to proceed?

Corporate culture sets the tone. A circumspect approach is to follow the lead; bending the rules can await the stage when you are sure of your ground. In some organisations it is said that employees don't speak to anyone other than those at their own level in the hierarchy, let alone calling the senior partner 'Len'. Then again, a member of the Cabinet may well be addressed jovially on a telly chat show, by his or her first name, but in official dealings it will be 'Minister' and don't you forget it. Distance and deference according to the incumbent's appointment, rank or post is advisable in styles of address at the work place.

I'm top dogsbody round here.

The tricky part is knowing where the limits lie. Among the few certainties is that an assumption of intimacy is always discourteous.

Newcomers and those on unsure ground are advised to do their homework on the house codes before embarking on a matey mode. Sources of guidelines for the uninitiated include the organisation's notice boards, any in-house literature left lying about, and gossip in the loos, as well as noticing what the others do.

It is always acceptable to ask authority how it would care to be addressed, with no offence given. But there are circumstances in which an admission of uncertainty might give an undesirable impression and seem naive or inexperienced.

In practice, boundaries to equality in nomenclature have a habit of popping up unexpectedly: the senior who seems happy enough to be on christian name terms with all and sundry on his or her own territory has been known to take umbrage when the personnel in the room changes. Chummy attitudes of junior staff may not go down so well with the boss in the presence of his or her own superior, or in front of an important client or VIP.

A sign that the use of a friendly style wouldn't be frowned upon is if the employer or department head is of a generation to have fond recollections of his hippy days. Exaggerated politeness or reference to 'Sir' might prove disquieting to him for any number of reasons. One to follow where close associates lead.

Your Ten-Thirty

A visiting fireman with an appointment should be met, greeted and cordially received. The important point is for the newcomer to be reassured that the people who should be made aware of his or her arrival are informed of the fact. There is usually suspicion on the part of all but VIP visitors that they are about to be kept waiting because no one has been informed of their arrival.

If the person who is calling is delayed in getting to their appointment, the polite action would be to let the people they are calling on know, and not to assume that time is the oyster of others.

On the other hand, if a visitor is about to be kept waiting, the same applies. On this point, what might be refreshing is for whoever is charged with the task of explaining away the delay, to spare the recipient the usual euphemisms such as, 'He will be with you in five minutes' or 'She is running very late today'. Yet absolute honesty might smack of disloyalty to the company. Better to apologise briefly and say as little as possible, making a point of promising to return in no time to keep the person in touch with developments.

General rules are that visitors may be asked to leave their coat or park any belongings, and be offered a chair. The offer of a cup of tea or coffee, even if this is the best that the office machine can provide, shows consideration.

A guideline on introductions between strangers is that the person who initiated the meeting, introduces himself or herself first. Otherwise, the member on home territory does the honours, making introductions all round. It is impolite to allow visitors to remain unattended and to fail to introduce them to members of staff in their orbit.

A ploy for ending a meeting that has extended its usefulness for the person in control is to say something along the lines of 'Well, we mustn't keep you any longer from your (fill in suitable reference: return journey ... next appointment ...)', followed by briskly rising to the feet and extending a hand of farewell. When a set period of time for the appointment has been established, of course, that is an acceptable cover, following a glance at the wristwatch.

A handshake, by the way, can be close and confident, but a bone cruncher seems a form of retaliation.

On The Line

The telephone, in addition to being a miracle of communication, is also a supreme cause of personal friction. Telephonic contact always promises so much so easily that when users are thwarted, they resent the shortfall. No doubt one other reason why the irritation stakes reach such a high in office life is that calls tend to be tension-laden. Results may hang on a few seconds of conversation down the line.

Making full allowances for the ambivalent position of many takers and makers of calls, a more courteous approach all round would reduce the number of times in which users feel put off, put down or put out. The following touches on some widely-shared irritants, both as sins of omission and commission.

- Promising to ring back and failing to do so.
- Being unnecessarily slow on the uptake to answer a ringing telephone.
- Allowing a colleague's telephone to ring unattended.
- Leaving callers on a silent line indefinitely without cutting in to let them know their call is being attended to.
- Redirecting incoming callers to an extension without checking that someone is available to take their call.
- Inaccurately scribbling down messages intended for colleagues.
- Refusal to accept responsibility (as the instigator of the call) for calling back when a conversation is prematurely disconnected by the switchboard.
- Neglecting to give a personal name or the name of a department when answering a call.
- Uttering excuses to callers that no longer wash such as 'He's still in a meeting' or 'I don't expect her back in the office today', or 'She is with the supervisor' without offering to take a message or proffering help.
- Omitting to mollify a caller whose attempts to contact a party were deflected by any of the above ploys with ameliorating remarks such as 'Can I ask him to call you back later?', or suggesting 'I'll try and interrupt her at her meeting'.

*I'm here to engage you in light
conversation while you're on hold.*

● Asking a secretary to put through a call to someone on your behalf, in which the person who is being rung is obliged to hang about until the instigator of the call decides to pick up the telephone.
● Adopting a synthetically breezy tone of voice in which to announce the name of the company or department.
● Demanding as a visitor to an office to use the company line before even exchanging greetings.
● Making or receiving long calls in the presence of a visitor on a matter which has no connection with them.
● Making the assumption that when a female voice at the surgery answers the call to Dr Brown, she must be the secretary.

It is not by chance that the decision to give someone a bell at work could produce a sufficient number of adverse reactions to fill this entire little book.

Dear Answering Machine

Difficult as it is to imagine a business world without the answering machine, few would deny that a spot of human consideration would transform the system way beyond the dreams of technology. The small robot seems to tempt users to be inconsiderate.

Why on earth should callers who ask for their call to be returned fail to leave call-back information, as so frequently occurs? Address files are incomplete, memories short and those who hope for a response might remember to record both a telephone number and a contact name for the convenience of the person rung.

Similarly, diallers are reminded of the frustrations likely to be caused by the Call That Never Was. When changing your mind about leaving a message, it is kind to refrain from waiting until the signal to speak, before ringing off. If you linger silently on the line, the play-back listener may be obliged to speculate on whether that long silence followed by bleeps represents a routine call, some nutcase or all that remains of a juicy commission.

Not everyone is competent at recording a long and complicated message impromptu. There is nothing against going through what has to be said in the head, before committing the performance to tape. As a general

Anyone here expecting a fax from an 'angelbum'?

rule, however, lengthy recorded messages are an imposition on grounds of hogging finite tape time, risking denying subsequent callers the opportunity to record their message.

Such a convenient medium of communication would seem a natural for issuing and acknowledging business invitations and the like. In the majority of cases, probably so, but where it is important to give a specially good impression the means might seem over-casual. Messages can be wiped inadvertently and may not always be delivered to the right quarters. A play-safe approach would confine the machine to confirming arrangements made in person or by letter, telephone or fax.

Similarly in the case of thank-you letters. A written

note or person-to-person exchange seems likely to convey a greater degree of appreciation than a recorded message. Incidentally, users of fax machines may follow suit.

Among general caveats in the use of both systems is the danger of communicating confidential information which might go public, and of course of transmitting communications likely to embarrass or offend the subject if stumbled upon by interested parties. Callers' general rules for business are to leave a name, the date and time of the call and a call-back number.

Owners of answering machines could mend their ways too. Recording an outgoing message in a friendly voice but one that is not assertively bright, will have a better chance of a good reception. Also, this may be some compensation to a caller for being fobbed off with a disembodied voice instead of the person called.

The owner's message, however minimal and guarded in the interests of security, should contain what is needed to confirm that the caller has reached base. A telephone number or department or company name seems basic.

Smoking Issues

Hoping to escape the eye of the boss in order to enjoy a surreptitious smoke has been part of working life for years. What has changed is the increasing difficulty of lighting up without causing offence, now that the anti-smoking lobby has gained widespread public support.

Trying to find a workable compromise that might enable X, who regards a puff of tobacco smoke as a personal affront, to rub along with Y, to whom lighting up a cigarette is regarded as one of life's precious freedoms, calls for near-saintly tolerance and awareness on all sides.

Courtesy can help. Sensitive points concern those many situations and circumstances in which smoking remains at the discretion of the individual. It could be at a social do beyond the no-smoking caveat, in a private office, or when entertaining a client in a restaurant.

One eventuality that is difficult to deal with without resorting to heavy-handedness, is that of the regular desk mate who cheerfully ignores the official no-smoking embargo and lights up as a matter of course. When space has to be shared, falling back on official complaints may well be counter-productive and merely sour the air in another way.

Looking at the matter from a smoker's viewpoint, he or she may feel deprived of their own life-saver or at least of a chance to break the monotony.

A liberal approach might be to turn a blind eye to the occasional lapse, but to look and sound discomfited if the person continues to take advantage. Coughing may cause

*I'm not going to jump, I've just come out
for a smoke.*

a twinge of conscience, particularly if this is recognised for the coded warning it is.

Should the lover of the weed seek collusion in their wish to bend the rules, few would think it impolite for a request to smoke to be refused. It would be nice if the refusal was accompanied by a tacit apology, however.

What could encourage the smoker to retire for a break might be the offer to make absence less of an inconvenience for them. Offering to man his/her telephone, take messages and if necessary to keep them in touch with any news of import, might make the move more attractive.

Smokers who hope to get away with things might

think to smoke in a considerate manner. Spent matches, ash and stubs can be disposed of sooner rather than later. Pipes of tobacco can be emptied with due caution. Smoke-filled spaces should be ventilated where possible. Smoke can be blown away from, instead of unconcernedly directed at, others. This similarly applies as a courtesy between fellow smokers, as does the repayment in kind from borrowers.

A general rule is that when someone's good will is being sought, it is no bad thing to consider his or her views on the matter of smoking. For instance, it would show consideration when booking a table for a client who is an avowed anti-smoker, to choose a restaurant with a no-smoking area.

Should a meeting take place in one of the few private offices excluded from a no-smoking ban, it nevertheless would be polite for members to ask permission to smoke before lighting up. If the chief whose den it is lights up, it is reasonable to assume that others may follow suit.

A last word concerns employers' attitudes to the employment of lovers of the weed. Many now stipulate a non-smoker for certain posts. In addition, managements may take the view that smoking habits are indicative of personal discipline. One such breach might be being seen smoking in the street. Eyebrows among the hierarchy may be raised even higher if the culprit is female, unfair as this may be.

Staff Jolly

Big wigs, old hands and new favourites are assured of a smooth ride at the staff party. The rest are renownedly liable to feel as if they have put their foot in it in some way. The combination of edgy bonhomie, drink, power-broking, to say nothing of the chance of romance or sexual adventure, is enough to make anyone wonder how to stay clear of the tripwires. A few of the hazards are explored below.

What might be seen as 'negative behaviour' could often be redeemed if loners would try to join in. The party-shy, and this applies to those who don't care for collective jollifications on principle, would find sounder camouflage in plunging in and avoiding standing on the sidelines in an outsider stance. One of the advantages of the gathering is that it is acceptable for members to nobble each other, whatever their relative place on the company perch may be. Even so, few subordinates have the bottle to buttonhole their department head or superior unsupported. A friendly intermediary might make the connection. Needless to add, such a meeting is rarely the right moment to raise the issues that are in the forefront of your mind, such as an increase in salary, the grim working conditions in your office, or the hopeless performance of your marketing manager.

Suggesting topics of conversation in this context is

usually spurious, but what can be said is that brown-nosing, with all the sycophancy implied, can redound to the discredit of the perpetrator. If compliments are to be paid, the art lies in finding good reasons for the gesture.

An encounter with the high-ups could be an opportunity to introduce yourself as an individual, detached for once from the occupational pigeon-hole in which you are usually confined.

Team-mates with a sociable approach will break away for the duration, and resist the temptation to remain in a huddle continuing the unfinished harangue back at work. Anyone feeling lost or lonely can keep an eye out for fellow strays, and will most likely be thanked for their pains. Candour prompts the reminder to be wary about befriending the no-hopers to the exclusion of the up-and-comers.

Looking confident is half the battle. This is especially true of any member who for one reason or another believes he or she is in a down position. The approach may well confound any detractors.

Knowing the code of arrival and departure times can be a particular advantage. Putting in a super-punctual appearance, say five minutes after the appointed hour, may win an early bird a chance of a chat to the host — an opportunity that could be lost when the crowds swarm in.

A seriously belated arrival calls for an apology and a watertight excuse. If large numbers of guests are in-

Mr. Smith will indicate the right people to be seen talking to.

volved it may be possible to slip in unnoticed, but the chances are that authority will spot the ruse and a *faux pas* will be compounded. Apologies should be kept short and snappy at the time.

Leaving conspicuously early also calls for a brief apology and explanation. Baby or parental problems, travel hold-ups, any cause in the interests of duty, are likely to be acceptable. A respectable hour at which to take your leave is when the signal is given to close the bar, or a short while before the stipulated cut-off hour on the invitation.

It is always courteous to make an effort to find the host to say goodbye and thanks, though it can be tactless to intrude on an animated conversation between chief and client or a big wheel associate. The same might be said of interrupting a blossoming emotional alliance.

Written thank-yous are unusual for inter-office dos, but visitors might think to take the trouble.

Dos and Don'ts

Sparing a thought for the members of the gathering might transform company dos in no time at all. In place of the somewhat heart-sinking prospect that attends much official business hospitality, the invitation might even lift the spirits. Making full allowances for the mix of business and pleasure, a lot more could be done to jolly up a branch of entertaining that often seems to defeat its objectives. Pulling this one off is less a matter of the budget than of the social skills of the host or organiser, spending time and effort on planning the event, and showing a willingness to put some heart into the agenda.

Everything depends, naturally, but an interesting choice of location is one way of breaking out of the mould of everydayness. Routine is a known quencher of the party spirit. The venue might even provide visitors with a treat in its own right. The gathering might take place in a building or grounds of special interest, aboard a boat, at an ice rink or swimming pool, or simply be held in a pleasant room somewhere accessible.

Introducing a few fresh faces from other walks who are likely to enhance the mix is another device for stimulating the company. Such might be local prominent people or those of standing in the world of the organisation concerned, or even a few lively friends of the host's, who might stir things profitably.

An understanding of contemporary food and drink tastes is more than courteous. The option of vegetarian dishes is par for the course in much business entertaining, and this might be combined with allowances for other food requirements – bearing practicalities in mind. If numbers are involved, invitees could specify dietary requirements on a reply card; if a small gathering, by word of mouth.

Smoking, that great divider, also needs to be taken into account if people are to enjoy themselves. Not easy. One approach where space permits is to provide a separate zone for smokers: smoking on social occasions has always been hedged with limits.

Very probably, managements will take the view that if a no-smoking embargo applies generally at the workface, it would be the majority wish for the party to abide by the restriction too. However, if the do is held at a venue outside the firm's premises, or out of doors or where smoking is generally accepted, as at a dinner dance for example, it might seem officious to insist on 'no-smoking'.

How much drink? Some balance has to be struck between stinginess and irresponsible liberality in the light of drink-drive laws, for one thing. A good bottle will never go unnoticed among wine bibbers. Soft drinks, mineral water and non-alcoholic beverages need not be boring, and the host's consideration will be noted.

Many a company do is far from immune from problems connected with members' marital state of affairs. Invitations are simple when a colleague is solidly married, but what of long-standing unofficial relationships between singles, or extra-marital liaisons within the band of gold? Custom favours adding 'and guest' to single's invitations, where this suits, or addressing separate invitations to staffer and boyfriend or girlfriend. In cases in which someone is married yet has a publicly-recognised unofficial partner, a general ruling is inappropriate. Much depends on the approach of the management and the associate's own wishes in the matter. It goes without saying that at a mixed do, the usual course is to invite an employee with his or her spouse, irrespective of the state of their private relationship.

As to table seating plans, spouses or members and their guests are seated together as a rule, on the basis that, as one of the couple may feel among strangers, he or she will be comforted in finding a familiar figure as a neighbour.

The seating plan is inevitably the making or breaking of conversation, and requires diplomacy to ensure that the wife of the sales rep who has been passed over for promotion is not seated beside the young Turk who won the day.

Hosts are urged to play that role. It is friendly to welcome everyone as they arrive and to circulate afterwards. If time and the set-up allows, guests up and down the hierarchy appreciate a chance to talk to the host. At a sit-down do, the practice of drawing up a chair for a few minutes at different tables shows interest.

Diversions and entertainments as part of the programme are an honoured and popular way of uniting a disparate audience. If sexy romps are envisaged of the 'kissogram' order, some care has to be exercised to ensure that things don't go a smooch too far.

The idea of hosting a do to which members' families are invited is a winning one — and repays the back-up teams at home. Ideas might include a visit to a theme park, a fun fair, a concert, or a firm favourite is a competitive sports day with events for the youngest visitors and most senior members.

No!

Office celebrations and Christmas parties would not be what they are without some gossipy happening between the sexes. The office Lothario, as likely as not unaccompanied by regular girlfriend or spouse, chances his arm on sexual conquest.

Women, understandably, have ceased to be amused by these caprices, which thinly disguise a demeaning

Look out – he's doing his mating display.

view of their sex. In addition, a woman may well object to being chatted up libidinously by members of the opposite sex, with the underlying assumption that these advances are welcome to her.

Politic is for the lady to use the skills of her sex for keeping control of men, and to try to prevent any incident from getting out of control or going too far. Good humour, diplomacy and tact can be put to good use. More precisely, she might stress an exciting new emotional interest in her life or talk up a jealous spouse.

My Apologies

The bulldog breed has no great reputation for making apologies – if we discount British Rail. In affairs between individuals, we seem to prefer silence to saying sorry. A pity, this, because knowing when an apology is due is as effective a way of smoothing ruffled feathers in working life as it is elsewhere.

In imbroglios involving hurt or wounded feelings, for example, the old rule obtains. The sooner an apology is made, the better. Done face to face is the braver course, and may spark an extra note of respect in the breast of the offended-against party. Failing this — not always possible if the fracas is between people of unequal status in the hierarchy — a written note should be sent marked 'Confidential' or 'For the Attention of' the wounded party. Ideally, the missive should be spared the public exposure of in-tray delivery. Privacy is of the essence in apologies, and for this reason the convenience of the fax machine, answering machine or message system via a personal computer should be eschewed. An exception would be in the case of apologising for a minor mishap.

Composing a spoken or written apology depends on the gravity of the offence, but some general points apply: never grovel as it is demeaning to both parties; avoid rubbishing a colleague; refrain from repeating the remark that caused the offence; regrets should always be ungrudging; and sincerity will carry more conviction than fine phrases. Sometimes a simple comment to the effect that you are sorry for what happened and would like to apologise is all that need be said.

Face-saving tactics (very much depending) might draw on the excuse that you were too close to the detail to see the overall pitfalls ahead; that you misunderstood the orders; that the remarks were intended humorously and had been misinterpreted. A personal background to a lapse of performance might help: bad news, domestic upset, low state of health. Care should be taken not to overplay the compassionate card, and one personal excuse only will suffice. Circumstances such as believing one is being discriminated against or victimised will call for stronger measures, but hints could be dropped in any apology.

A caveat to the above is that apologising officially for bad service, mistakes or errors in a business or professional context may have serious implications. This applies particularly when you are apologising to another company if a bad error has been made: your job could be jeopardised in any admission of liability.

That's no excuse for failing to apologise if you are in the wrong on the human side. Regrets may be expressed without admitting responsibility. Once again, this is all a question of the manner in which things are done.

Excuses

Office life would be too painful to contemplate without excuses for arriving late and leaving early. It seems fair therefore in this epilogue, to bend the rules a little and advise wage slaves where they stand. A sex bias may be discernible as far as acceptability by authority is concerned.

A man's good luck in this respect is that he may be exonerated on grounds of a 'lapse', whereas a woman's misfortune is that similar behaviour may provoke mutterings about her ability to get herself together.

The following examples of excuses are grouped by gender into those that invite the benefit of the doubt and those that risk causing opprobrium. Far from watertight, these probably depend for acceptance as much on the sex of the jury as on the justification.

ACCEPTABLE EXCUSES FOR MEN

Late night out with the boss
Tickets for the big match
Broken window at party
Appointment for hair cut
Shopping for female secretary's birthday present.
Mislaid car keys

ACCEPTABLE EXCUSES FOR WOMEN

Sponsored charity run
Taking car to be serviced
Gas leak at home
Vet appointment for 'Patch'
Taking offspring to doctor
Attendance at offspring's school play

DODGY EXCUSES FOR MEN

Amorous exhaustion
Moped packed up
Granny's funeral
House-hunting
Late at gym
Attendance at offspring's school play

DODGY EXCUSES FOR WOMEN

Late night out with the boss
Broken window at party
P.M.S. (pre-menstrual syndrome)
Shopping for female secretary's birthday present
Baby sitter delayed
Mislaid car keys